Epic Cars

BMW i8

MEGAN COOLEY PETERSON

BLACK RABBIT BOOKS

Bolt is published by Black Rabbit Books
P.O. Box 3263, Mankato, Minnesota, 56002.
www.blackrabbitbooks.com

Jen Besel, editor; Grant Gould, designer;
Omay Ayres, photo researcher

Library of Congress Cataloging-in-Publication Data
Names: Peterson, Megan Cooley, author.
Title: BMW I8 / Megan Cooley Peterson.
Description: Mankato, Minnesota : Black Rabbit Books, 2021. | Series: Bolt. Epic cars | Includes bibliographical references and index. | Audience: Ages 8-12 | Audience: Grades 4-6 | Summary: "Experience what it's like to be behind the wheel of a BMW i8 through exciting text, vibrant photography, and labeled images and other graphics"— Provided by publisher.
Identifiers: LCCN 2019027603 (print) | LCCN 2019027604 (ebook) | ISBN 9781623102555 (hardcover) | ISBN 9781644663516 (paperback) | ISBN 9781623103491 (ebook)
Subjects: LCSH: BMW automobiles—Juvenile literature.
Classification: LCC TL215.B25 P48 2021 (print) | LCC TL215.B25 (ebook) | DDC 629.222/2—dc23
LC record available at https://lccn.loc.gov/2019027603
LC ebook record available at https://lccn.loc.gov/2019027604

Printed in the United States. 4/20

Image Credits

Alamy: Oldtimer, 31; autotrader.com: Autotrader, 19 (b); autozone.com: Auto Zone, 3; bmw-sg.com: BMW.SG, 32; bmwblog.com: 28–29; bmwi.bimmerpost.com: BMW i8 Forum, 1; bmwusa.com: BMW i8, 4–5, 6, 12–13, 16, 18, 21, 23 (t), 24, 26–27 (main); BMW i8 Coupe, 26 (t); hiveminer.com: Automotive Rhythms, 10–11; Media.torqeedo.com: Torqeedo, 23 (b); motor1.com: AC Schnitzer, 8–9; press.bmwgroup.com: BMW Group PressClub, Cover (car); BMW Group, 14–15, 17, 19 (t); Shutterstock: Elenamiv, Cover (bkgd)

Contents

CHAPTER 1

Racing Down the Road

A BMW i8 shoots down the road. Its engine howls as it zooms around a corner. Its sleek body has a cutting-edge look. The car races from 0 to 60 miles (97 kilometers) per hour in just 4.2 seconds.

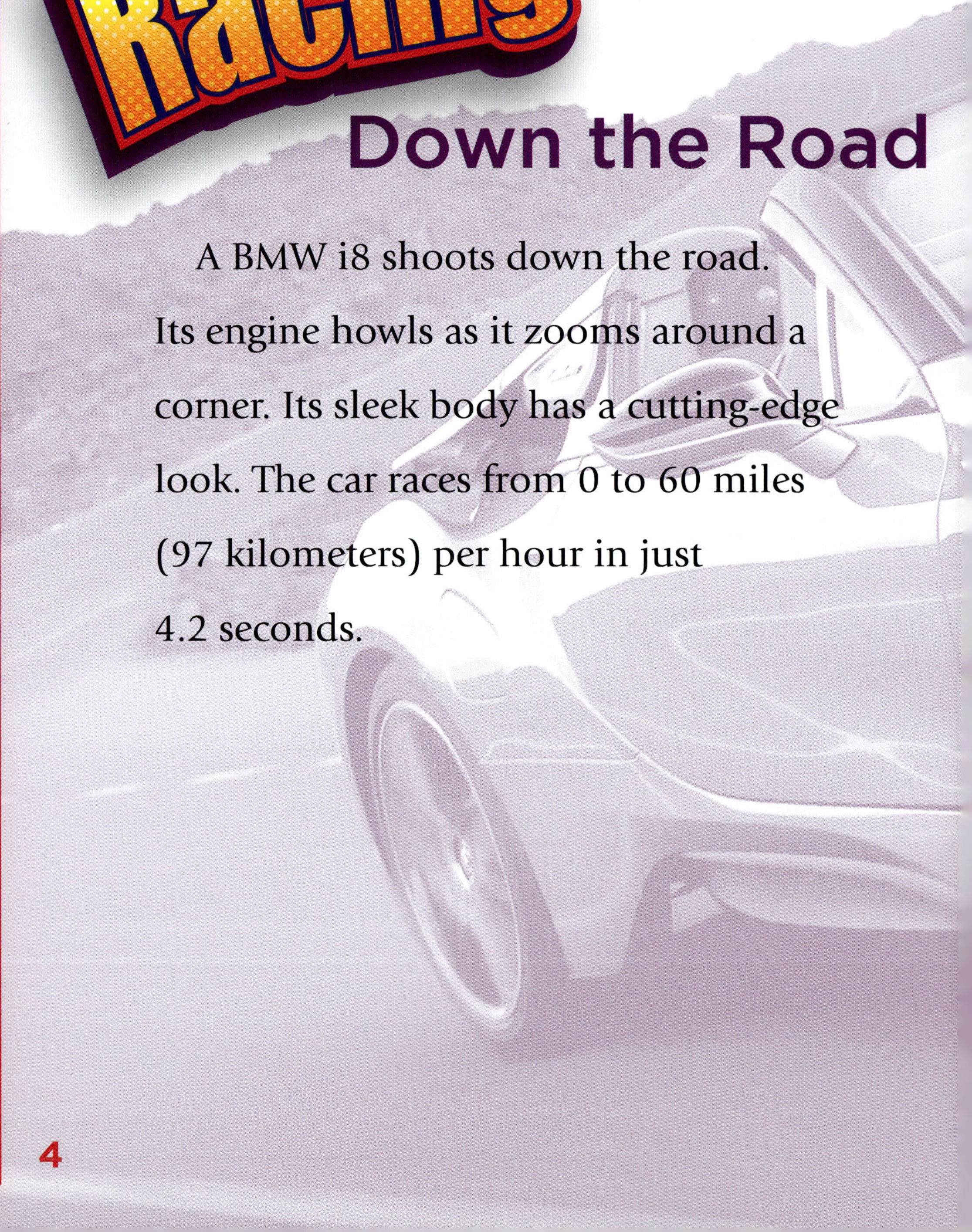

Timeline of i8's Development

2008

BMW starts Project i to design and build electric cars.

2009

The i8 concept car is unveiled.

A New Sports Car

BMW **unveiled** the i8 in 2013. The car didn't just look cool. It was also doing something new. It ran on both gas and electricity. It was one of the first **hybrid** sports cars.

2013
The first i8 production car is revealed.

2014
The first i8 is sold to the general public.

2019
The 2019 i8 is unveiled. It has a larger battery.

PARTS OF A BMW i8

SMOOTH BODY
GRILLE
AC I 8001
AIR CHANNELS

CHAPTER 2

Design

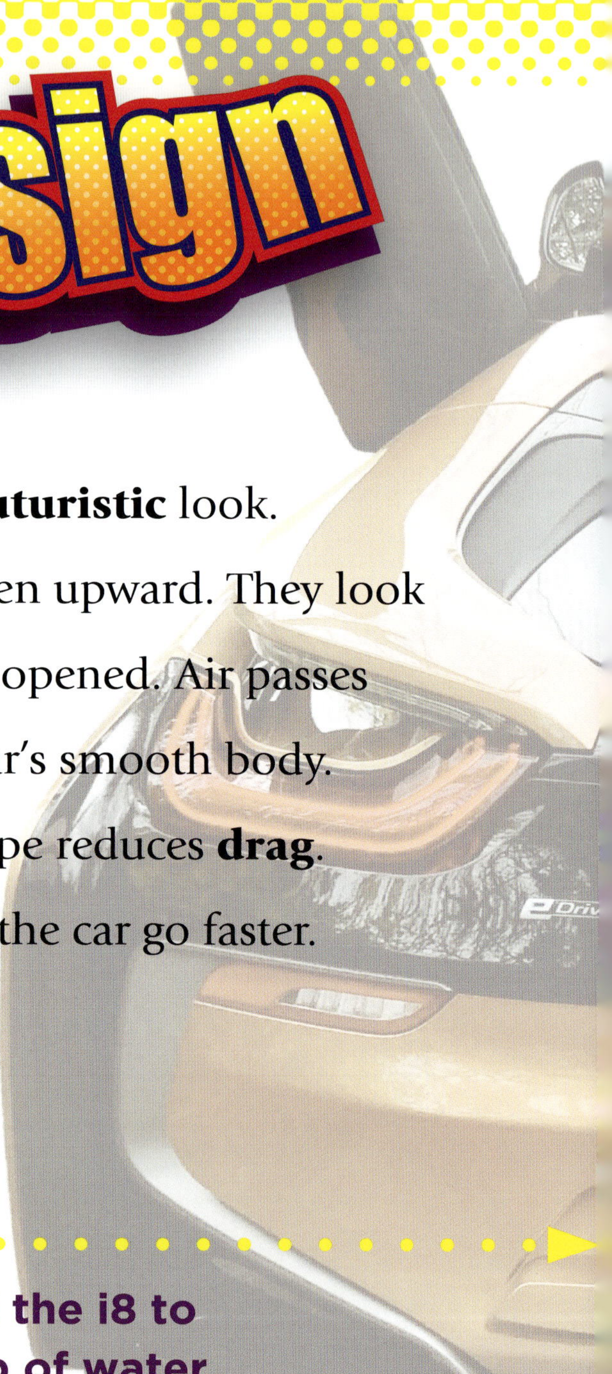

The i8 has a **futuristic** look. Scissor doors open upward. They look like wings when opened. Air passes easily over the car's smooth body. This smooth shape reduces **drag**. Less drag makes the car go faster.

BMW designed the i8 to look like a drop of water.

BMW
i8

Body Frames

Most cars have a single frame. But not the i8. It has two separate body frames. The passenger frame is made of plastic and **carbon fiber**. These materials keep the car light. They also keep passengers safer.

The drive frame is made of **aluminum**. It houses the car's battery, motor, and engine. Having two frames leaves more room for passengers.

i8 BODY FRAMES

PASSENGER FRAME

ConnectedDrive
Wetter heute in Yaiza
22 / 35°C
Mein Fahrzeug
ePOWER
COMFORT
0
km/h
MODE
AIRBAG
SYNC
20.5°
AUTO
START STOP
eDRIVE
SPORT

Interior

The i8's stylish design continues in the interior. Its clean look is trimmed in carbon fiber. Leather seats have built-in warmers. A display screen lets drivers control maps and music. The screen can also display whatever is on the driver's phone.

The i8's key fob has a touch screen. Drivers can swipe to lock their car and check gas levels.

Personalized

Buyers can personalize their i8s. They can choose between a **coupe** and convertible. The i8 comes in six colors and three wheel choices. Buyers can also choose from four interior colors.

Wheel Choices

BI-COLOR WHEELS

W-SPOKE WHEELS

JET BLACK WHEELS

CHAPTER 3

Power and Performance

The BMW i8 is paving the way for hybrid supercars. An electric motor sits under the hood. A twin-turbo gas engine sits at the back. The weight is spread evenly to keep the car balanced. When in hybrid mode, the car uses both gas and electricity.

front electric motor

Electric Power

A battery powers the i8's electric motor. It sits between the electric motor and gas engine. The motor puts out 141 horsepower. Combined with the engine, the i8 has 369 horsepower.

The i8's battery fully charges in about three hours.

FUEL ECONOMY

2019 BMW i8 (hybrid mode)

2019 Acura NSX

2019 DBS Superleggera

---

miles per gallon

Driving Modes

BMW i8 drivers can choose from four driving modes. Each mode changes the way the car handles. The fully electric mode uses no gas. In this mode, the car reaches 75 miles (121 km) per hour. The convertible i8 can travel about 33 miles (53 km) on electric power alone.

Fuel economy is how far a vehicle goes on one gallon of gas.

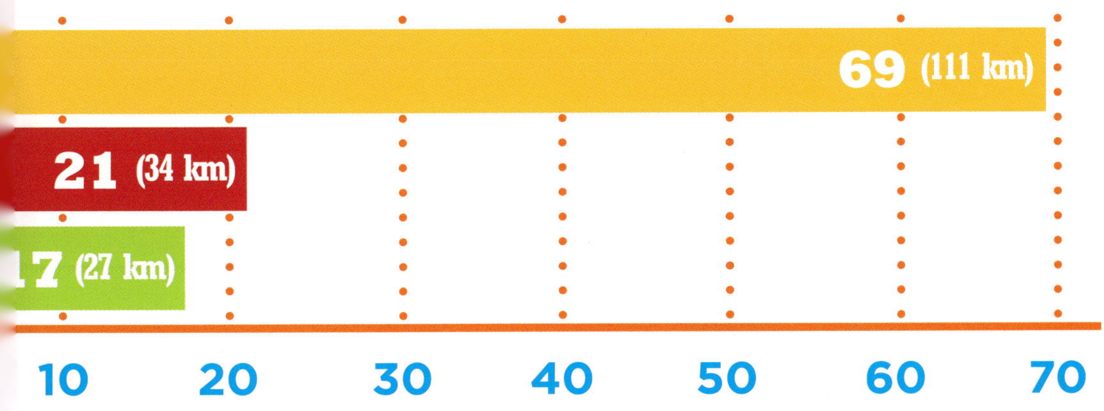

By the Numbers

more than **44,000** battery charging stations worldwide

$163,300
BASE PRICE OF THE 2019 CONVERTIBLE

155
miles (250 km) per hour

TOP SPEED OF THE i8

FD 5476

CHAPTER 4

An Epic Car

BMW is known for making epic cars. The i8 is no exception. This supercar combines power with good fuel economy. Buyers love driving in style with this awesome car.

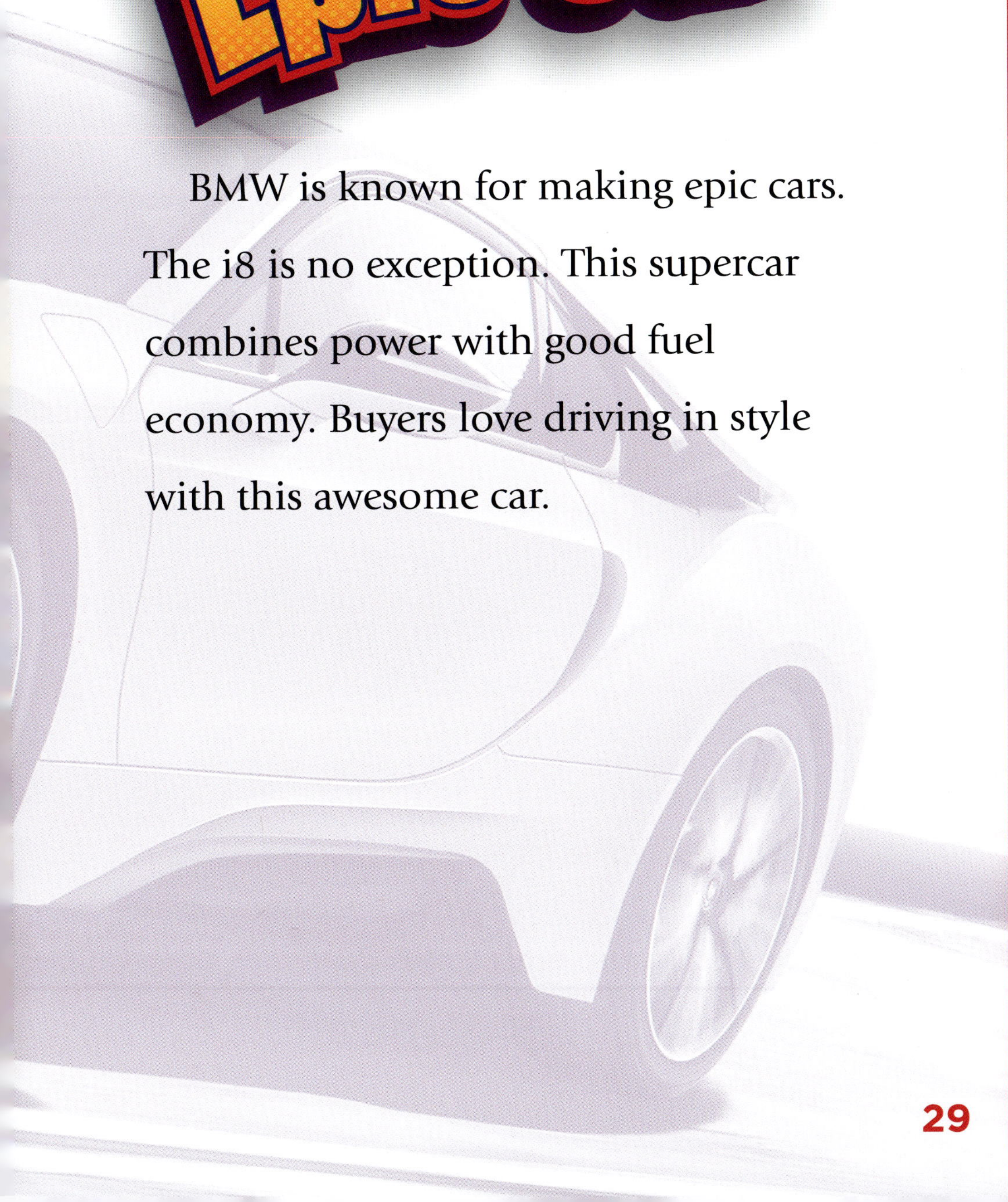

aluminum (uh-LOO-mih-num)—a silver-white light metallic chemical element that is easily worked

carbon fiber (KAR-buhn FAHY-bur)—a very strong, lightweight material

coupe (KOOP)—a two-door automobile

drag (DRAYG)—something that makes action or progress slower or more difficult

futuristic (fyoo-chuh-RIS-tik)—advanced or very modern

grille (GRIL)—a mesh framework covering at the opening at the front of a car

hybrid (HI-brid)—something, such as a vehicle, that has two different types of components performing essentially the same function

key fob (KEY FAHB)—a small electronic device used typically in place of a key, as to unlock a door or start a vehicle

unveil (un-VAYL)—to make public

LEARN MORE

BOOKS

Fishman, Jon M. *Cool Sports Cars*. Awesome Rides. Minneapolis: Lerner Publications, 2019.

Garstecki, Julia. *Corvette Z06*. Epic Cars. Mankato, MN: Black Rabbit Books, 2020.

Niver, Heather Moore. *21st Century Cars*. Feats of 21st Century Engineering. New York: Enslow Publishing, 2019.

WEBSITES

2019 BMW i8 Review, Pricing, and Specs
www.caranddriver.com/bmw/i8

BMW i8 Coupe and i8 Roadster
www.bmwusa.com/vehicles/bmwi/bmw-i8.html

History
www.bmwgroup.com/en/company/history.html

INDEX